JUNIOR SONGSCAPE

EARTH, SEA AND SKY

25 original songs for classroom
and concert use

LIN MARSH

with CD

 FABER *ff* MUSIC

ACKNOWLEDGEMENTS

These songs were commissioned by the Culm Valley Small Schools Association as part of their 'Planet Earth' arts project and were first performed in the Great Hall, Exeter University 10th July 2004.

© 2004 by Faber Music Ltd
First published in 2004 by Faber Music Ltd
Bloomsbury House
74–77 Great Russell Street
London WC1B 3DA
Cover design by Shireen Nathoo Design
Music processed by Jeanne Fisher
Printed in England by Caligraving Ltd

ISBN10: 0-571-52206-8
EAN13: 978-0-571-52206-4

CD recorded in Rectory Studio, High Wycombe, May 2004
Voice: Lin Marsh (and Kathryn Oswald); Piano: John Lenehan
Engineer: John Lenehan; Producer: Kathryn Oswald
℗ 2004 Faber Music Ltd © 2004 Faber Music Ltd

To buy Faber Music publications or to find out about the full range of titles available please contact your local music retailer or Faber Music sales enquiries:

Faber Music Limited, Burnt Mill, Elizabeth Way, Harlow, CM20 2HX England
Tel: +44 (0)1279 82 89 82   Fax: +44 (0)1279 82 89 83
sales@fabermusic.com   fabermusic.com

PREFACE

This set of twenty-five songs was originally composed for a cluster of small primary schools in east Devon as part of a year's arts project on 'Planet Earth'. The Sea songs are aimed at years 1 and 2, the Earth songs at years 3 and 4 and the Sky songs for years 5 and 6. The whole set stands as a complete school project or you could dip in and out as in a conventional songbook.

The songs are arranged progressively in the book both in the lyrics and the music. Simple part-singing is introduced in section 2 and developed in section 3, but for the less confident is of course optional. When teaching simple part-songs, it can be a good idea to let one half hum their part quietly, helping the others learning the new bit to keep in time and give them a sense of key. You may find pupils who would like to sing a solo verse or sing in a small group. Do encourage them to do this – it is great for confidence, and often very effective for a first verse.

Always warm up voices and faces before a singing session (see *The Show Must Go On!*) and encourage the pupils to experiment with different voice qualities and dynamics to make the songs really come alive.

'Planet Earth' was a wonderful commission to work on – the scope for creating different atmospheres through lyrics and musical style was exciting and challenging. You will find here lyrical, humorous, stately and mysterious songs – even a hornpipe and a blues. Do have fun adding movement or dramatizing them and don't feel too bound by the suggested age ranges. Enjoy!

Lin Marsh, May 2004

CONTENTS

Big boats, small boats

Lin Marsh

Pirates!

Lin Marsh

1: The
2: The
3: They're

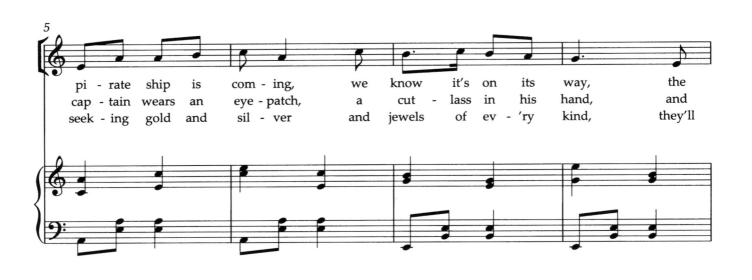

pi - rate ship is com - ing, we know it's on its way, the
cap - tain wears an eye - patch, a cut - lass in his hand, and
seek - ing gold and sil - ver and jewels of ev - 'ry kind, they'll

pi - rate ship is com - ing, we've seen it in the bay.
on the bridge be - side him, his faith - ful pi - rates stand. A
board each sail - ing ves - sel and take what they can find.

skull and cross-bones on the mast, a wild and noi-sy crew: the___

pi-rate ship is com-ing and it's af-ter me and you!

Yo-ho-ho and a bot-tle of rum, pi-rates like to have their fun!

Yo-ho-ho on the 'Sal-ty Breeze' as they sail the se-ven seas. seas.

Playing on the beach

Lin Marsh

1: I've

packed my buck - et, packed my spade, I've sun - cream ev - 'ry -
cas - tle's built, I've dug a hole to let the wa - ter
tide's gone out, the sun's gone down, but I don't mind at

- where. We've packed a sand - wich, packed a drink, and
through. I've bu - ried Dad be - neath the sand and
all – I've walked a - long the pro - me - nade and

Gran - ny's fold - ing chair._____
had an ice - cream too._____ I'm feel - ing so ex - ci - ted,___ I
played with bat and ball._____

The rock pool

Lin Marsh

In a rock style

1: Oh we like to play in the
(2:) big rock pool and there's
(3:) - lect - ed sea - weed,_____
(4:) bet - ter rush or we'll

rock pool on the shore,_____
room for ev - 'ry - one,_____
ra - zor shells and sand,_____
ne - ver beat the tide,_____

oh we like to play in the
it's a big rock pool and there's
we've col - lect - ed sea - weed,_____
oh we'd bet - ter rush or we'll

The lighthouse

Lin Marsh

through the dark - ness, shine out clear and bright, ___

shine out with your mes - sage, guid - ing the ships, ___

bring - ing them home, ___ safe when they see ___ your light.

light.

Seagull

Lin Marsh

We're going swimming

7

Lin Marsh

Underwater

Lin Marsh

1: Un - der - wa - ter there's a
2: Un - der - wa - ter there's a
3: Un - der - wa - ter where the

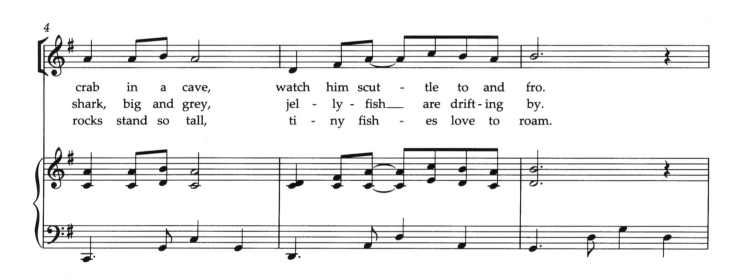

crab in a cave, watch him scut - tle to and fro.
shark, big and grey, jel - ly - fish___ are drift - ing by.
rocks stand so tall, ti - ny fish - es love to roam.

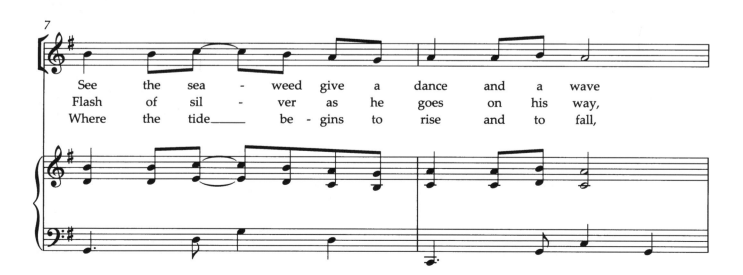

See the sea - weed give a dance and a wave
Flash of sil - ver as he goes on his way,
Where the tide___ be - gins to rise and to fall,

Desert

Lin Marsh

Slow and hot!

The dinosaur gang

Lin Marsh

crea - tures ap - peared on the scene.
liked to meet up just for lunch.
brain power was all they had right.
end of the di - no - saur gang.

There was Bron - to - sau - rus,

Al - lo - sau - rus, Di - plo - do - cus too, Bra - chio - sau - rus,

Ste - go - sau - rus, just to name a few. Some were big and

some were small, some were ti - ny, some were tall— all part of the

di - no - saur gang!   gang!

1., 2., 3.   4.

Mighty glacier

Lin Marsh

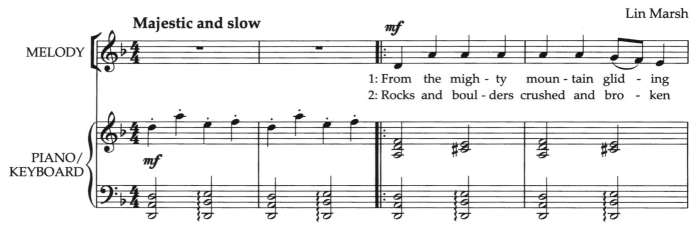

strong.

3: Though you shim-mer as you're flow-ing,
4: From the migh-ty moun-tain glid-ing

snow and ice are all you're show-ing, carv-ing out the path you're mak-ing,
comes the fro-zen ri-ver slid-ing, creak-ing, squeak-ing, slow and stea-dy,

cer-tain of the way you're tak-ing.
melt-ing in the sun al-rea-dy.

Migh-ty gla-cier

state-ly, slow, born so ma-ny years a-go, migh-ty gla-cier jour-ney on,

no-ble, proud and strong.

River journey

Lin Marsh

1: Un - der the ground there are
2: Through the green mea - dows it
3: Then come the ra - pids with

bub - bles and splash - es, then down the hill - side the lit - tle stream
swirls and me - an - ders, on past the sheep and the cat - tle it
twist - ing and turn - ing, o - ver the rocks and the stones it is

dash - es. This way and that way it tum - bles with glee,
wan - ders. Flow - ing through reeds where the ducks make their nest,
churn - ing. Out to the o - cean it wan - ders at last,

Mountain air

Lin Marsh

15

climb - ing to the ve - ry top, where the snow is
peo - ple walk - ing in the woods, peo - ple on their
where the goat - herd guards his flock, hear the yo - d'llers

18

1, 2.   3.   mf

bright.
skis!   sing!   We're all off for some

21

moun - tain air,   yo - de - lo - de - lay,   yo - de - lo - de - lee,

24

come and join us__ if you dare,   yo - de - lo - de - lay, yo - de - lee.

The rainforest

Lin Marsh

1: Hum - ming birds are search - ing for some nec - - tar,
2: Mon - keys chat - ter loud - ly in the tree tops
3: See the pret - ty par - rot and the tou - - can,

bees are buzz - ing all day long.
play - ing games of hide and seek,
what a bright - ly co - loured pair,

But - ter - flies are dan - cing in the morn - ing sun,___
Jump - ing on each o - ther as they chase a - round,___
Fly - ing off to find a lit - tle snack or two,___

spi - der spins his web so ve - ry strong.
e - ven ar - ma - dil - lo has a peek!___ *The*
poor old Mis - ter Bee - tle: do take care!___

1., 2.

The swamp

Lin Marsh

and big,   sharp teeth   are   rea - dy   to   bite   in the
and   you   can   hear   a   ter - ri - ble   crunch   in the
you've   seen   e - nough,   it's   time   to   get   out   of   the

hid - den   from   sight,
time   for   their   lunch,
shift - ing   a - bout,

swamp.
swamp.
swamp.

mp

in   the   swamp.
in   the   swamp.
of   the   swamp.

1., 2.   *mp*   3.

2: It's
3: Your

f

There's a rumbling and a rolling

Lin Marsh

With a real rock 'n' roll feel

1: There's a rum - bling___ and a
2: There's a boil - ing___ and a
3: All the ash flies___ as the

roll - ing___ as the ground be - gins___ to shake,___ And a
bub - bling___ as we hear his pow - er - ful snore,___ Then the
giant sighs___ and the sky grows grey___ and dark,___ And the

grum - bling___ and a groan - ing___ as the earth be - gins___ to quake,___
moun - tain___ gives a shud - der,___ when he wakes up with__ a roar.___
heat grows___ as the hill glows___ like the migh - ty gi - ant's heart.___

And a cra - ter o - pens wide___ where the
As the la - va starts to__ flow___ all the
There are rum - bles from the__ deep___ till at

migh - ty gi - ant hides___ in the vol - ca - no.___
hill - side is a - glow___ on the vol - ca - no.___
last he falls a - sleep___ in the vol - ca - no.___

repeat twice

f

I am the wind

Lin Marsh

Aliens!

Lin Marsh

1: A - li - ens,___ we are a - li - ens___ and we've
2: A - li - ens,___ though we're a - li - ens___ we are
3: A - li - ens,___ call us a - li - ens,___ for our

tra -velled for light years to vi - sit you here. A - li - ens,___ friend - ly
speak-ing your lan - guage the best that we can. A - li - ens,___ an - cient
looks are un - u -sual we quite re - a - lise. A - li - ens,___ though we're

a - li - ens,___ our in - ten -tions are peace -ful, you've no -thing to fear.
a - li - ens,___ we were ru - lers of space long be -
a - li - ens___ please don't judge on ap - pear -ance – we're real - ly quite wise.

Hot-air balloon

Lin Marsh

PIANO/ KEYBOARD

Andante

mp legato

con Ped.

PART 1

Would - n't you like to go float - ing_____ high in a

PART 2

Would - n't you like to go float - ing?_____

beau - ti - ful bal - loon?_____ Drift - ing with ease,

_____ Here it's so beau - ti - ful a - drift - ing with ease,

go where you please high in your co - loured bal - loon._____

go where you please high in your co - loured bal - loon._____

1., 2.

46

Space travel

Lin Marsh

10

out - er space,_____
me - te - ors,_____
sa - tel - lite,_____

float - ing through the hea - vens you'll be
hop - ing you may find a place to
jour - ney - ing a - cross the dark - est

12

free.
stay.
sky.

f

Belt - up,
Weight - less,
Hav - ing

it's time for
you're in a
a great ad -

14

take - off,_____
space - suit,_____
- ven - ture,_____

count - ing down, count - ing down:
breath - ing out, breath - ing in,
spin - ning round, not a sound,

16

three, two,_____ one!_____
float - ing_____ free._____
far from_____ home._____

En - gines flash - ing on your
As you whoosh a - cross the
Stars are twink - ling as you

Communication

Lin Marsh

14 now we com-mu-ni-cate a-cross the e-ther,__ boun-cing our mes-sa-ges from

17 out-er space.__ Sa-tel-lites soon beam in-for-ma-tion,__

20 di-gi-tal tech-no-lo-gy all a-round the place!

verse 3 to Coda 1.

mp

2: We

23 2.

mp

E-mail, ra-di-o, mo-bile, mes-sa-ging,

mp

52

T. V.,   in - ter - net,   fly - ing through the air.

Sound - waves,   mi - cro - waves,

so - nar, sa - tel - lite – com - mu - ni - ca - tion is   ev - 'ry - where!

D. S. 𝄋 *al* 𝄌
then to Coda   𝄌 CODA
mp

3: We

mp   *p*

Gravity!

Lin Marsh

14 (ALL)

gives you weight, it keeps your din - ner on the plate.
- wards the earth, though you may fight for all you're worth. With -
- on the ground, it stops us fly - ing up and down.

17

- out it where would we all__ be?__ Let's be grate - ful__ for

20 *Fine* mp

gra - vi - ty!__ Just i - ma - gine what would hap - pen__ if we

23

all float - ed round in space: bump - ing, jump - ing

D. S. 𝄋 al Fine

Silver moon

Lin Marsh

3rd time to Coda

1: An - cient vol - ca - noes and moun - tains stand high, cra - ters and
2: Mov - ing a - round us your out - line we see, chang - ing your

rocks wide-ly flung._____ Though you've been spin - ning for
shape night by night._____ Pull - ing our tides as you

bil - lions of years, you still give us light from the
or - bit the earth, you glow with a ma - gi - cal

poco rit. *repeat twice* **CODA** **molto rall.**

dim.

sun._____
light._____

Stars

Lin Marsh

Moving along

MELODY

PIANO/
KEYBOARD

1: Ti - ny dots of light, spar - kl - ing and bright,
2: Drift - ing through this space, each must have a place

light the dark - est hea - vens when the night is clear.
fol - low - ing a jour - ney des - ti - ny has planned.

Pat - terns fill the sky — charts to guide us by,
So we gaze in awe, learn - ing more and more,

con Ped.

shin - ing there be - fore us, seem - ing oh so near.
wish - ing for a mo - ment we could un - der - stand.

Earth, sea and sky

Lin Marsh

Lyrics:

1: Have you ev-er danced a-cross a mead-ow on a warm and sun-ny sum-mer's
2: Have you watched a per-fect lit-tle snow-flake as it floats so soft-ly down to
3: Have you ev-er list-ened to a black-bird as he sings his song for all to

day? Or list-ened to the rus-tle as the wind flies by, or
land? Or tried to catch a sun-beam as it falls to earth, or
hear? Or watched the break-ers rush-ing to the san-dy shore, or

smelt the scent of new-mown hay?
held a sea-shell in your hand? Take a mo-ment,
count-ed stars as they ap-pear?

LYRICS

Big boats, small boats

Big boats, small boats, any kind at all boats,
Who knows where they're going 'cross the deep, blue sea?
Big ships, tall ships, any kind at all ships,
Sailing to and fro across the deep, blue sea.

1 Pedal in a pedal boat, paddle a canoe,
  Fish upon a fishing boat – catch a fish or two!

Big boats, small boats …

2 Motor on a motor boat, sail upon a yacht,
  Row a little rowing boat, tie a sailor's knot!

Big boats, small boats …

3 See the mighty ferries pass, heavy tankers too,
  Coloured flags upon the mast: red and white and blue!

Big boats, small boats …

Pirates!

1 The pirate ship is coming,
  We know it's on its way,
  The pirate ship is coming,
  We've seen it in the bay.
  A skull and crossbones on the mast,
  A wild and noisy crew:
  The pirate ship is coming
  And it's after me and you!

Yo-ho-ho and a bottle of rum,
Pirates like to have their fun!
Yo-ho-ho on the 'Salty Breeze'
As they sail the seven seas.

2 The captain wears an eye-patch,
  A cutlass in his hand,
  And on the bridge beside him,
  His faithful pirates stand.
  A skull and crossbones on the mast …

Yo-ho-ho and a bottle of rum …

3 They're seeking gold and silver
  And jewels of ev'ry kind,
  They'll board each sailing vessel
  And take what they can find.
  A skull and crossbones on the mast …

Yo-ho-ho and a bottle of rum …

Playing on the beach

1 I've packed my bucket, packed my spade,
  I've suncream ev'rywhere.
  We've packed a sandwich, packed a drink,
  And Granny's folding chair.
  I'm feeling so excited, I love to go away,
  We're visiting the seaside: my fav'rite place to play.

I've got sand in my fingers, sand in my toes,
Sand in my hair and sand in my clothes,
Sand in my nails and sand up my nose (at-choo!)
But I love to play on the beach!

2 The castle's built, I've dug a hole
  To let the water through.
  I've buried Dad beneath the sand
  And had an ice-cream too.
  I'm feeling so excited …

I've got sand in my fingers …

3 The tide's gone out, the sun's gone down,
  But I don't mind at all –
  I've walked along the promenade
  And played with bat and ball.
  I'm feeling so excited …

I've got sand in my fingers …

The rock pool

1 Oh we like to play in the rock pool on the shore,
  Oh we like to play in the rock pool on the shore,
  Well we've caught three crabs
    but we'd like to catch one more!

2 It's a big rock pool and there's room for ev'ryone,
  It's a big rock pool and there's room for ev'ryone,
  Well the water's warm and we're having lots of fun!

3 We've collected seaweed, razor shells and sand,
  We've collected seaweed, razor shells and sand
  And a limpet I just can't get off my hand!

4 Oh we'd better rush or we'll never beat the tide,
  Oh we'd better rush or we'll never beat the tide,
  Now our bucket's full and the rock pool's all inside!
  Yeah!

The lighthouse

1 On the cliff a lighthouse stands, straight and tall,
  Flashing out across the sea, warning all.

Shine out through the darkness,
Shine out clear and bright,
Shine out with your message,
Guiding the ships, bringing them home,
Safe when they see your light.

2 On the cliff a lighthouse stands, white and red
  Flashing out across the sea: 'Rocks ahead!'

Shine out through the darkness …

3 From the top a beacon glows, night and day,
  Flashing out across the sea: 'Keep away!'

Shine out through the darkness …

Seagull

Seagull, oh seagull please take me with you
High over cliff-tops and oceans so blue,
Watching the waves and the dolphins at play –
Seagull, oh seagull let's both fly away!

Soaring and gliding, dipping and diving,
Blown by the wind we'll fly far out to sea,
Rising and falling, swooping and calling,
Blown by the wind, oh how happy we'll be.

Seagull, oh seagull …

We're going swimming

1 The sand is warm, the sky is blue,
  It all seems so exciting.
  The sun is out, enjoy the view,
  The water looks inviting.

One, two, three – we're going swimming,
Take a breath and dip your toe,
One, two, three – we're going swimming:
Start to shiver, all of a quiver,
Knees start to shake, what a mistake!
Fingers turn blue, so do you,
Why is it so cold? Let's be bold!
One, two, three, four, five, six, seven!
Splash! It's heaven!

2 Across the sand you make your way,
  It all seems so exciting.
  You paddle at the water's edge,
  The sea looks so inviting.

One, two, three ….

Underwater

1 Underwater there's a crab in a cave,
  Watch him scuttle to and fro.
  See the seaweed give a dance and a wave
  As the tide begins to flow.

Underwater is a world to explore,
There the fish are swimming free.
Treasures lying on the ocean floor,
Pretty shells for you and me.

2 Underwater there's a shark, big and grey,
  Jellyfish are drifting by.
  Flash of silver as he goes on his way,
  Little fish all give a sigh.

Underwater is a world to explore …

3 Underwater where the rocks stand so tall,
  Tiny fishes love to roam.
  Where the tide begins to rise and to fall,
  Crab and lobster make their home.

Underwater is a world to explore …

Desert

Hot, dry, dusty sand, desert land.
Sky and mirage meet, desert heat.
Dunes shift grain by grain back again.
No shade, no air, desert bare.

Mist is rising in this silent place,
Stone and rock reflect the sun,
Of a shadow there is not a trace, empty space.

Hot, dry, dusty sand …

The dinosaur gang

1 A long time ago when this planet was new,
  It all looked quite diff'rent to me and to you.
  And long before humans had started to dream,
  Some very strange creatures appeared on the scene.

There was Brontosaurus, Allosaurus, Diplodocus too,
Brachiosaurus, Stegosaurus, just to name a few.
Some were big and some were small,
Some were tiny, some were tall –
All part of the dinosaur gang!

2 They roamed through the forest,
  They ran 'cross the plain,
  They fought with each other again and again.
  Their claws and their teeth made it easy to crunch,
  And all of them liked to meet up just for lunch.

There was Brontosaurus …

3 They built giant nests where their eggs then were laid,
  And hung out together within the green glade.
  They liked to pretend they were gifted and bright:
  But muscle not brain power was all they had right.

There was Brontosaurus …

4 Then sadly they all disappeared one by one –
  Some said it was due to the light of the sun.
  But some said a meteor had crashed with a bang
  And hasten'd the end of the dinosaur gang.

There was Brontosaurus …

Mighty glacier

1 From the mighty mountain gliding
Comes the frozen river sliding,
Creaking, squeaking, slow and steady,
Melting in the sun already.

2 Rocks and boulders crushed and broken
Just as if a giant's awoken,
Bright and white your jagged edges,
Dark and deep your mountain ledges.

Mighty glacier stately, slow,
Born so many years ago,
Mighty glacier journey on,
Noble, proud and strong.

3 Though you shimmer as you're flowing,
Snow and ice are all you're showing,
Carving out the path you're making,
Certain of the way you're taking.

4 From the mighty mountain gliding
Comes the frozen river sliding,
Creaking, squeaking, slow and steady,
Melting in the sun already.

Mighty glacier …

River journey

1 Under the ground there are bubbles and splashes,
Then down the hillside the little stream dashes.
This way and that way it tumbles with glee,
Jumping and flashing so glad to be free.

The river's journey starts with a spring,
Where the skylark sings happy and free.
From mountain and hillside through valley it flows
And ends with the call of the sea.

2 Through the green meadows it swirls and meanders,
On past the sheep and the cattle it wanders.
Flowing through reeds where the ducks make their nest,
On to the mill pond to stop for a rest.

The river's journey …

3 Then come the rapids with twisting and turning,
Over the rocks and the stones it is churning.
Out to the ocean it wanders at last,
Hearing the call as the seagull flies past.

The river's journey …

Mountain air

We're all off for some mountain air,
Yo-de-lo-de-lay, yo-de-lo-de-lee,
Come and join us if you dare,
Yo-de-lo-de-lay, yo-de-lee.

1 On the lift or cable car – what a lovely sight,
Climbing to the very top where the snow is bright.

We're all off …

2 I can see for miles around – houses, lakes and trees,
People walking in the woods, people on their skis!

We're all off …

3 See the pretty mountain flowers, hear the cowbells ring,
Where the goatherd guards his flock,
    hear the yod'llers sing!

We're all off …

The rainforest

The rainforest breathes and the rainforest sighs
And the trees turn their leaves to the sun.
With colours so bright, smell the scent in the air,
See the flowers open up, one by one.

1 Humming birds are searching for some nectar,
Bees are buzzing all day long.
Butterflies are dancing in the morning sun,
Spider spins his web so very strong.

The rainforest breathes …

2 Monkeys chatter loudly in the tree tops
Playing games of hide and seek,
Jumping on each other as they chase around,
Even armadillo has a peek!

The rainforest breathes …

3 See the pretty parrot and the toucan,
What a brightly coloured pair,
Flying off to find a little snack or two,
Poor old Mister Beetle: do take care!

The rainforest breathes …

The swamp

1 A swamp's a strange and mysterious place,
Of anything living there's hardly a trace,
But eyes are watching, though hidden from sight,
And big sharp teeth are ready to bite in the swamp.

2 It's dark and dangerous, muddy and damp,
With crocodiles lining each side of the bank.
Their tummies rumble, it's time for their lunch,
And you can hear a terrible crunch in the swamp.

3 Your feet are sinking, you're holding on fast,
For ten pairs of eyes have moved silently past,
And strange, new shadows are shifting about –
You've seen enough, it's time to get out of the swamp.

There's a rumbling and a rolling

1 There's a rumbling and a rolling
As the ground begins to shake,
And a grumbling and a groaning
As the earth begins to quake,
And a crater opens wide where the mighty giant hides
In the volcano.

2 There's a boiling and bubbling
As we hear his powerful snore,
Then the mountain gives a shudder,
When he wakes up with a roar.
As the lava starts to flow all the hillside is a-glow
On the volcano.

3 All the ash flies as the giant sighs
And the sky grows grey and dark,
And the heat grows as the hill glows
Like the mighty giant's heart.
There are rumbles from the deep
Till at last he falls asleep
In the volcano.

I am the wind

1 You'll hear me rattle on the windowpane,
You'll hear me rustle in the leaves,
You'll feel me blowing through the open door,
You'll see me bend the mighty trees.

For I am the wind, I am invincible,
I come and go just as I please.
I am the wind, I am invisible,
I come and go
Yet nobody sees.

2 I bring the ice from cold Siberia,
And from the Arctic send the snow.
I'll warm you with the hot Sahara sand,
Or from the west the rain I'll blow.

For I am the wind …

3 At times I turn into a hurricane
And travel far across the sea,
I'll twist and turn with all the strength I have,
And set the mighty oceans free.

For I am the wind …

Aliens!

1 Aliens, we are aliens
And we've travelled for light years to visit you here.
Aliens, friendly aliens,
Our intentions are peaceful, you've nothing to fear.

PT 1 *Bee-dle-ee-dle-eep, beep, beep,*
      Bee-dle-ee-dle-eep, beep, beep,
      Bee-dle-ee-dle-eep, beep, beep, beep!

PT 2 *brrrr, brrrr, brrrr, brrrr!*

PT 3 *beep, beep beep,*
      beep beep, beep beep,
      beep beep, beep beep, beep beep!

2 Aliens, though we're aliens
We are speaking the language the best that we can.
Aliens, ancient aliens,
We were rulers of space long before the big bang.

PTS   For millions of years we have tapped out our signals,
1&2   For millions of years we have studied the skies.
      But here you are sitting on your little planet,
      No wonder you seemed to get such a surprise!

PT 3 *Ah …*

3 Aliens, call us aliens,
For our looks are unusual we quite realise.
Aliens, though we're aliens
Please don't judge on appearance –
    we're really quite wise.

PT 1 *Bee-dle-ee-dle-eep, beep, beep …*

PT 2 *brrrr, brrrr, brrrr, brrrr.*

PT 3 *beep beep, beep beep …*

4 Aliens, yes we're aliens,
There's a far better world waiting out there for you.
Aliens, yes we're aliens,
But we think you should listen, there's so much to do!

Hot-air balloon

PT 1 *Wouldn't you like to go floating*
      High in a beautiful balloon?
      Drifting with ease, go where you please
      High in your coloured balloon.

PT 2 *Wouldn't you like to go floating?*
      Here it's so beautiful
      A-drifting with ease, go where you please
      High in your coloured balloon.

1 Over the hills and the valleys,
Over the rivers and trees,
Peaceful and calm as you travel,
Following each little breeze.

Wouldn't you like to go floating …

2 Swaying high up in your basket,
Patchwork the fields lie below.
Watching the distant horizon,
Lit by the sun's warming glow.

Wouldn't you like to go floating …

Lifting, gently drifting, holding on tight
As you conquer the skies.
Riding, gently gliding, winging your way
Where the eagle flies.

Wouldn't you like to go floating …

Space travel

1 Would you like to travel on a spaceship
To a distant galaxy?
Whizzing through the atmosphere to outer space,
Floating through the heavens you'll be free.
Belt-up, it's time for take-off,
Counting down, counting down: three, two, one!
Engines flashing on your rocket ship,
You'll be having so much fun!

2 Would you like to travel on a spaceship
Right across the Milky Way?
Whizzing past the asteroids and meteors,
Hoping you may find a place to stay.
Weightless, you're in a spacesuit,
Breathing out, breathing in, floating free.
As you whoosh across the universe
You'll be making history!

3 Would you like to travel on a spaceship?
At the speed of light you'll fly.
Sending out your messages by satellite,
Journeying across the darkest sky.
Having a great adventure,
Spinning round, not a sound, far from home.
Stars are twinkling as you hurry by,
Maybe you are not alone!

PT 1 | Would you like to travel on a spaceship,
Would you like to travel on a spaceship – free?

PT 2 | Would you like to travel on a spaceship,
Would you like to travel out so free?

Communication

1 We used to beat drums to send a message,
Playing out patterns on skin and wood.
We used to light fires, blow smoke to signal
Telling our neighbours what news we could.

But now we communicate across the ether,
Bouncing our messages from outer space.
Satellites soon beam information,
Digital technology all around the place!

2 We used to tie notes to carrier pigeons,
Waiting and hoping they'd find their way.
We used to use light to send in Morse code,
Semaphore signals across the bay.

But now we communicate …

Email, radio, mobile, messaging,
T.V., internet, flying through the air.
Sound-waves, microwaves, sonar, satellite –
Communication is ev'rywhere!

3 We used to light beacons on the hill top,
Celebrate moments of history.
We used to fly flags on sailing vessels –
Colourful signals across the sea!

But now we communicate …

Gravity!

1 What keeps you lying in your bed at night?
It's gravity!
What stops the bed from drifting out of sight?
It's gravity!
It holds you down, it gives you weight,
It keeps your dinner on the plate.
Without it where would we all be?
Let's be grateful for gravity!

2 What keeps the table standing on the floor?
It's gravity!
What holds the pebbles on the rocky shore?
It's gravity!
It pulls you down towards the earth,
Though you may fight for all you're worth.
Without it where would we all be?
Let's be grateful for gravity!

Just imagine what would happen
If we all floated round in space:
Bumping, jumping through the atmosphere,
Gliding, sliding all around the place.
Just imagine what would happen
If we all landed on the moon:
Creeping, leaping through the atmosphere,
Springing, swinging like a big balloon, like a big balloon.

3 What keeps you sitting on your chair at school?
It's gravity!
What keeps the water in the paddling pool?
It's gravity!
It fastens us upon the ground,
It stops us flying up and down.
Without it where would we all be?
Let's be grateful for gravity!

Silver moon

Silver moon, soft and white,
Silver moon, shining bright.
Dappled on the water, shimmering through trees,
Riding the clouds on a breeze.

1 Ancient volcanoes and mountains stand high,
Craters and rocks widely flung.
Though you've been spinning for billions of years,
You still give us light from the sun.

Silver moon, soft and white …

2 Moving around us your outline we see,
Changing your shape night by night.
Pulling our tides as you orbit the earth,
You glow with a magical light.

Silver moon, soft and white …

Stars

1 Tiny dots of light, sparkling and bright,
Light the darkest heavens when the night is clear.
Patterns fill the sky – charts to guide us by,
Shining there before us, seeming oh so near.

Pleiades, Sirius, Gemini and Taurus,
Procyon, Canopus, grace us with your light.
Far across the Milky Way new galaxies are waiting,
Maybe while we're watching a new star shines tonight.

2 Drifting through this space, each must have a place
following a journey destiny has planned.
So we gaze in awe, learning more and more,
Wishing for a moment we could understand.

Pleiades, Sirius …

Earth, sea and sky

1 Have you ever danced across a meadow
On a warm and sunny summer's day?
Or listened to the rustle as the wind flies by,
Or smelt the scent of new-mown hay?

Take a moment, take your time
And never let this beauty pass you by.
This precious planet is a wonderful place:
The earth, the sea, the sky!

2 Have you watched a perfect little snowflake
As it floats so softly down to land?
Or tried to catch a sunbeam as it falls to earth,
Or held a seashell in your hand?

Take a moment …

3 Have you ever listened to a black bird
As he sings his song for all to hear?
Or watched the breakers rushing to the sandy shore,
Or counted stars as they appear?

Take a moment …